This password book belongs to:

_____

Published by SJ Books

A

Website:	
Date:	
Username:	
Password:	
Notes:	

Website:	
Date:	
Username:	
Password:	
Notes:	

Website:	
Date:	
Username:	
Password:	
Notes:	

Website:	
Date:	
Username:	
Password:	
Notes:	

A

Website:	
Date:	
Username:	
Password:	
Notes:	

Website:	
Date:	
Username:	
Password:	
Notes:	

Website:	
Date:	
Username:	
Password:	
Notes:	

Website:	
Date:	
Username:	
Password:	
Notes:	

A

Website:	
Date:	
Username:	
Password:	
Notes:	

Website:	
Date:	
Username:	
Password:	
Notes:	

Website:	
Date:	
Username:	
Password:	
Notes:	

Website:	
Date:	
Username:	
Password:	
Notes:	

Website:	
Date:	
Username:	
Password:	
Notes:	

Website:	
Date:	
Username:	
Password:	
Notes:	

Website:	
Date:	
Username:	
Password:	
Notes:	

Website:	
Date:	
Username:	
Password:	
Notes:	

B

Website:	
Date:	
Username:	
Password:	
Notes:	

Website:	
Date:	
Username:	
Password:	
Notes:	

Website:	
Date:	
Username:	
Password:	
Notes:	

Website:	
Date:	
Username:	
Password:	
Notes:	

Website:	
Date:	
Username:	
Password:	
Notes:	

Website:	
Date:	
Username:	
Password:	
Notes:	

Website:	
Date:	
Username:	
Password:	
Notes:	

Website:	
Date:	
Username:	
Password:	
Notes:	

B

Website:	
Date:	
Username:	
Password:	
Notes:	

Website:	
Date:	
Username:	
Password:	
Notes:	

Website:	
Date:	
Username:	
Password:	
Notes:	

Website:	
Date:	
Username:	
Password:	
Notes:	

B

Website:	
Date:	
Username:	
Password:	
Notes:	

Website:	
Date:	
Username:	
Password:	
Notes:	

Website:	
Date:	
Username:	
Password:	
Notes:	

Website:	
Date:	
Username:	
Password:	
Notes:	

C

Website:	
Date:	
Username:	
Password:	
Notes:	

Website:	
Date:	
Username:	
Password:	
Notes:	

Website:	
Date:	
Username:	
Password:	
Notes:	

Website:	
Date:	
Username:	
Password:	
Notes:	

Website:	
Date:	
Username:	
Password:	
Notes:	

Website:	
Date:	
Username:	
Password:	
Notes:	

Website:	
Date:	
Username:	
Password:	
Notes:	

Website:	
Date:	
Username:	
Password:	
Notes:	

C

Website:	
Date:	
Username:	
Password:	
Notes:	

Website:	
Date:	
Username:	
Password:	
Notes:	

Website:	
Date:	
Username:	
Password:	
Notes:	

Website:	
Date:	
Username:	
Password:	
Notes:	

Website:	
Date:	
Username:	
Password:	
Notes:	

Website:	
Date:	
Username:	
Password:	
Notes:	

Website:	
Date:	
Username:	
Password:	
Notes:	

Website:	
Date:	
Username:	
Password:	
Notes:	

D

Website:	
Date:	
Username:	
Password:	
Notes:	

Website:	
Date:	
Username:	
Password:	
Notes:	

Website:	
Date:	
Username:	
Password:	
Notes:	

Website:	
Date:	
Username:	
Password:	
Notes:	

Website:	
Date:	
Username:	
Password:	
Notes:	

Website:	
Date:	
Username:	
Password:	
Notes:	

Website:	
Date:	
Username:	
Password:	
Notes:	

Website:	
Date:	
Username:	
Password:	
Notes:	

D

Website:	
Date:	
Username:	
Password:	
Notes:	

Website:	
Date:	
Username:	
Password:	
Notes:	

Website:	
Date:	
Username:	
Password:	
Notes:	

Website:	
Date:	
Username:	
Password:	
Notes:	

D

Website:	
Date:	
Username:	
Password:	
Notes:	

Website:	
Date:	
Username:	
Password:	
Notes:	

Website:	
Date:	
Username:	
Password:	
Notes:	

Website:	
Date:	
Username:	
Password:	
Notes:	

E

Website:	
Date:	
Username:	
Password:	
Notes:	

Website:	
Date:	
Username:	
Password:	
Notes:	

Website:	
Date:	
Username:	
Password:	
Notes:	

Website:	
Date:	
Username:	
Password:	
Notes:	

E

Website:	
Date:	
Username:	
Password:	
Notes:	

Website:	
Date:	
Username:	
Password:	
Notes:	

Website:	
Date:	
Username:	
Password:	
Notes:	

Website:	
Date:	
Username:	
Password:	
Notes:	

E

Website:	
Date:	
Username:	
Password:	
Notes:	

Website:	
Date:	
Username:	
Password:	
Notes:	

Website:	
Date:	
Username:	
Password:	
Notes:	

Website:	
Date:	
Username:	
Password:	
Notes:	

Website:	
Date:	
Username:	
Password:	
Notes:	

Website:	
Date:	
Username:	
Password:	
Notes:	

Website:	
Date:	
Username:	
Password:	
Notes:	

Website:	
Date:	
Username:	
Password:	
Notes:	

F

Website:	
Date:	
Username:	
Password:	
Notes:	

Website:	
Date:	
Username:	
Password:	
Notes:	

Website:	
Date:	
Username:	
Password:	
Notes:	

Website:	
Date:	
Username:	
Password:	
Notes:	

F

Website:	
Date:	
Username:	
Password:	
Notes:	

Website:	
Date:	
Username:	
Password:	
Notes:	

Website:	
Date:	
Username:	
Password:	
Notes:	

Website:	
Date:	
Username:	
Password:	
Notes:	

F

Website:	
Date:	
Username:	
Password:	
Notes:	

Website:	
Date:	
Username:	
Password:	
Notes:	

Website:	
Date:	
Username:	
Password:	
Notes:	

Website:	
Date:	
Username:	
Password:	
Notes:	

F

Website:	
Date:	
Username:	
Password:	
Notes:	

Website:	
Date:	
Username:	
Password:	
Notes:	

Website:	
Date:	
Username:	
Password:	
Notes:	

Website:	
Date:	
Username:	
Password:	
Notes:	

G

Website:	
Date:	
Username:	
Password:	
Notes:	

Website:	
Date:	
Username:	
Password:	
Notes:	

Website:	
Date:	
Username:	
Password:	
Notes:	

Website:	
Date:	
Username:	
Password:	
Notes:	

Website:	
Date:	
Username:	
Password:	
Notes:	

Website:	
Date:	
Username:	
Password:	
Notes:	

Website:	
Date:	
Username:	
Password:	
Notes:	

Website:	
Date:	
Username:	
Password:	
Notes:	

G

Website:	
Date:	
Username:	
Password:	
Notes:	

Website:	
Date:	
Username:	
Password:	
Notes:	

Website:	
Date:	
Username:	
Password:	
Notes:	

Website:	
Date:	
Username:	
Password:	
Notes:	

G

Website:	
Date:	
Username:	
Password:	
Notes:	

Website:	
Date:	
Username:	
Password:	
Notes:	

Website:	
Date:	
Username:	
Password:	
Notes:	

Website:	
Date:	
Username:	
Password:	
Notes:	

Website:	
Date:	
Username:	
Password:	
Notes:	

Website:	
Date:	
Username:	
Password:	
Notes:	

Website:	
Date:	
Username:	
Password:	
Notes:	

Website:	
Date:	
Username:	
Password:	
Notes:	

Website:	
Date:	
Username:	
Password:	
Notes:	

Website:	
Date:	
Username:	
Password:	
Notes:	

Website:	
Date:	
Username:	
Password:	
Notes:	

Website:	
Date:	
Username:	
Password:	
Notes:	

Website:	
Date:	
Username:	
Password:	
Notes:	

Website:	
Date:	
Username:	
Password:	
Notes:	

Website:	
Date:	
Username:	
Password:	
Notes:	

Website:	
Date:	
Username:	
Password:	
Notes:	

Website:	
Date:	
Username:	
Password:	
Notes:	

Website:	
Date:	
Username:	
Password:	
Notes:	

Website:	
Date:	
Username:	
Password:	
Notes:	

Website:	
Date:	
Username:	
Password:	
Notes:	

Website:	
Date:	
Username:	
Password:	
Notes:	

Website:	
Date:	
Username:	
Password:	
Notes:	

Website:	
Date:	
Username:	
Password:	
Notes:	

Website:	
Date:	
Username:	
Password:	
Notes:	

Website:	
Date:	
Username:	
Password:	
Notes:	

Website:	
Date:	
Username:	
Password:	
Notes:	

Website:	
Date:	
Username:	
Password:	
Notes:	

Website:	
Date:	
Username:	
Password:	
Notes:	

Website:	
Date:	
Username:	
Password:	
Notes:	

Website:	
Date:	
Username:	
Password:	
Notes:	

Website:	
Date:	
Username:	
Password:	
Notes:	

Website:	
Date:	
Username:	
Password:	
Notes:	

Website:	
Date:	
Username:	
Password:	
Notes:	

Website:	
Date:	
Username:	
Password:	
Notes:	

Website:	
Date:	
Username:	
Password:	
Notes:	

Website:	
Date:	
Username:	
Password:	
Notes:	

J

Website:	
Date:	
Username:	
Password:	
Notes:	

Website:	
Date:	
Username:	
Password:	
Notes:	

Website:	
Date:	
Username:	
Password:	
Notes:	

Website:	
Date:	
Username:	
Password:	
Notes:	

J

Website:	
Date:	
Username:	
Password:	
Notes:	

Website:	
Date:	
Username:	
Password:	
Notes:	

Website:	
Date:	
Username:	
Password:	
Notes:	

Website:	
Date:	
Username:	
Password:	
Notes:	

J

Website:	
Date:	
Username:	
Password:	
Notes:	

Website:	
Date:	
Username:	
Password:	
Notes:	

Website:	
Date:	
Username:	
Password:	
Notes:	

Website:	
Date:	
Username:	
Password:	
Notes:	

Website:	
Date:	
Username:	
Password:	
Notes:	

Website:	
Date:	
Username:	
Password:	
Notes:	

Website:	
Date:	
Username:	
Password:	
Notes:	

Website:	
Date:	
Username:	
Password:	
Notes:	

K

Website:	
Date:	
Username:	
Password:	
Notes:	

Website:	
Date:	
Username:	
Password:	
Notes:	

Website:	
Date:	
Username:	
Password:	
Notes:	

Website:	
Date:	
Username:	
Password:	
Notes:	

K

Website:	
Date:	
Username:	
Password:	
Notes:	

Website:	
Date:	
Username:	
Password:	
Notes:	

Website:	
Date:	
Username:	
Password:	
Notes:	

Website:	
Date:	
Username:	
Password:	
Notes:	

K

Website:	
Date:	
Username:	
Password:	
Notes:	

Website:	
Date:	
Username:	
Password:	
Notes:	

Website:	
Date:	
Username:	
Password:	
Notes:	

Website:	
Date:	
Username:	
Password:	
Notes:	

Website:	
Date:	
Username:	
Password:	
Notes:	

Website:	
Date:	
Username:	
Password:	
Notes:	

Website:	
Date:	
Username:	
Password:	
Notes:	

Website:	
Date:	
Username:	
Password:	
Notes:	

L

Website:	
Date:	
Username:	
Password:	
Notes:	

Website:	
Date:	
Username:	
Password:	
Notes:	

Website:	
Date:	
Username:	
Password:	
Notes:	

Website:	
Date:	
Username:	
Password:	
Notes:	

L

Website:	
Date:	
Username:	
Password:	
Notes:	

Website:	
Date:	
Username:	
Password:	
Notes:	

Website:	
Date:	
Username:	
Password:	
Notes:	

Website:	
Date:	
Username:	
Password:	
Notes:	

L

Website:	
Date:	
Username:	
Password:	
Notes:	

Website:	
Date:	
Username:	
Password:	
Notes:	

Website:	
Date:	
Username:	
Password:	
Notes:	

Website:	
Date:	
Username:	
Password:	
Notes:	

L

Website:	
Date:	
Username:	
Password:	
Notes:	

Website:	
Date:	
Username:	
Password:	
Notes:	

Website:	
Date:	
Username:	
Password:	
Notes:	

Website:	
Date:	
Username:	
Password:	
Notes:	

M

Website:	
Date:	
Username:	
Password:	
Notes:	

Website:	
Date:	
Username:	
Password:	
Notes:	

Website:	
Date:	
Username:	
Password:	
Notes:	

Website:	
Date:	
Username:	
Password:	
Notes:	

Website:	
Date:	
Username:	
Password:	
Notes:	

Website:	
Date:	
Username:	
Password:	
Notes:	

Website:	
Date:	
Username:	
Password:	
Notes:	

Website:	
Date:	
Username:	
Password:	
Notes:	

Website:	
Date:	
Username:	
Password:	
Notes:	

Website:	
Date:	
Username:	
Password:	
Notes:	

Website:	
Date:	
Username:	
Password:	
Notes:	

Website:	
Date:	
Username:	
Password:	
Notes:	

Website:	
Date:	
Username:	
Password:	
Notes:	

Website:	
Date:	
Username:	
Password:	
Notes:	

Website:	
Date:	
Username:	
Password:	
Notes:	

Website:	
Date:	
Username:	
Password:	
Notes:	

Website:	
Date:	
Username:	
Password:	
Notes:	

Website:	
Date:	
Username:	
Password:	
Notes:	

Website:	
Date:	
Username:	
Password:	
Notes:	

Website:	
Date:	
Username:	
Password:	
Notes:	

Website:	
Date:	
Username:	
Password:	
Notes:	

Website:	
Date:	
Username:	
Password:	
Notes:	

Website:	
Date:	
Username:	
Password:	
Notes:	

Website:	
Date:	
Username:	
Password:	
Notes:	

Website:	
Date:	
Username:	
Password:	
Notes:	

Website:	
Date:	
Username:	
Password:	
Notes:	

Website:	
Date:	
Username:	
Password:	
Notes:	

Website:	
Date:	
Username:	
Password:	
Notes:	

N

Website:	
Date:	
Username:	
Password:	
Notes:	

Website:	
Date:	
Username:	
Password:	
Notes:	

Website:	
Date:	
Username:	
Password:	
Notes:	

Website:	
Date:	
Username:	
Password:	
Notes:	

Website:	
Date:	
Username:	
Password:	
Notes:	

Website:	
Date:	
Username:	
Password:	
Notes:	

Website:	
Date:	
Username:	
Password:	
Notes:	

Website:	
Date:	
Username:	
Password:	
Notes:	

O

Website:	
Date:	
Username:	
Password:	
Notes:	

Website:	
Date:	
Username:	
Password:	
Notes:	

Website:	
Date:	
Username:	
Password:	
Notes:	

Website:	
Date:	
Username:	
Password:	
Notes:	

Website:	
Date:	
Username:	
Password:	
Notes:	

Website:	
Date:	
Username:	
Password:	
Notes:	

Website:	
Date:	
Username:	
Password:	
Notes:	

Website:	
Date:	
Username:	
Password:	
Notes:	

Website:	
Date:	
Username:	
Password:	
Notes:	

Website:	
Date:	
Username:	
Password:	
Notes:	

Website:	
Date:	
Username:	
Password:	
Notes:	

Website:	
Date:	
Username:	
Password:	
Notes:	

P

Website:	
Date:	
Username:	
Password:	
Notes:	

Website:	
Date:	
Username:	
Password:	
Notes:	

Website:	
Date:	
Username:	
Password:	
Notes:	

Website:	
Date:	
Username:	
Password:	
Notes:	

P

Website:	
Date:	
Username:	
Password:	
Notes:	

Website:	
Date:	
Username:	
Password:	
Notes:	

Website:	
Date:	
Username:	
Password:	
Notes:	

Website:	
Date:	
Username:	
Password:	
Notes:	

Website:	
Date:	
Username:	
Password:	
Notes:	

Website:	
Date:	
Username:	
Password:	
Notes:	

Website:	
Date:	
Username:	
Password:	
Notes:	

Website:	
Date:	
Username:	
Password:	
Notes:	

P

Website:	
Date:	
Username:	
Password:	
Notes:	

Website:	
Date:	
Username:	
Password:	
Notes:	

Website:	
Date:	
Username:	
Password:	
Notes:	

Website:	
Date:	
Username:	
Password:	
Notes:	

Q

Website:	
Date:	
Username:	
Password:	
Notes:	

Website:	
Date:	
Username:	
Password:	
Notes:	

Website:	
Date:	
Username:	
Password:	
Notes:	

Website:	
Date:	
Username:	
Password:	
Notes:	

Q

Website:	
Date:	
Username:	
Password:	
Notes:	

Website:	
Date:	
Username:	
Password:	
Notes:	

Website:	
Date:	
Username:	
Password:	
Notes:	

Website:	
Date:	
Username:	
Password:	
Notes:	

Q

Website:	
Date:	
Username:	
Password:	
Notes:	

Website:	
Date:	
Username:	
Password:	
Notes:	

Website:	
Date:	
Username:	
Password:	
Notes:	

Website:	
Date:	
Username:	
Password:	
Notes:	

Website:	
Date:	
Username:	
Password:	
Notes:	

Website:	
Date:	
Username:	
Password:	
Notes:	

Website:	
Date:	
Username:	
Password:	
Notes:	

Website:	
Date:	
Username:	
Password:	
Notes:	

Website:	
Date:	
Username:	
Password:	
Notes:	

Website:	
Date:	
Username:	
Password:	
Notes:	

Website:	
Date:	
Username:	
Password:	
Notes:	

Website:	
Date:	
Username:	
Password:	
Notes:	

Website:	
Date:	
Username:	
Password:	
Notes:	

Website:	
Date:	
Username:	
Password:	
Notes:	

Website:	
Date:	
Username:	
Password:	
Notes:	

Website:	
Date:	
Username:	
Password:	
Notes:	

Website:	
Date:	
Username:	
Password:	
Notes:	

Website:	
Date:	
Username:	
Password:	
Notes:	

Website:	
Date:	
Username:	
Password:	
Notes:	

Website:	
Date:	
Username:	
Password:	
Notes:	

R

Website:	
Date:	
Username:	
Password:	
Notes:	

Website:	
Date:	
Username:	
Password:	
Notes:	

Website:	
Date:	
Username:	
Password:	
Notes:	

Website:	
Date:	
Username:	
Password:	
Notes:	

S

Website:	
Date:	
Username:	
Password:	
Notes:	

Website:	
Date:	
Username:	
Password:	
Notes:	

Website:	
Date:	
Username:	
Password:	
Notes:	

Website:	
Date:	
Username:	
Password:	
Notes:	

S

Website:	
Date:	
Username:	
Password:	
Notes:	

Website:	
Date:	
Username:	
Password:	
Notes:	

Website:	
Date:	
Username:	
Password:	
Notes:	

Website:	
Date:	
Username:	
Password:	
Notes:	

S

Website:	
Date:	
Username:	
Password:	
Notes:	

Website:	
Date:	
Username:	
Password:	
Notes:	

Website:	
Date:	
Username:	
Password:	
Notes:	

Website:	
Date:	
Username:	
Password:	
Notes:	

Website:	
Date:	
Username:	
Password:	
Notes:	

Website:	
Date:	
Username:	
Password:	
Notes:	

Website:	
Date:	
Username:	
Password:	
Notes:	

Website:	
Date:	
Username:	
Password:	
Notes:	

T

Website:	
Date:	
Username:	
Password:	
Notes:	

Website:	
Date:	
Username:	
Password:	
Notes:	

Website:	
Date:	
Username:	
Password:	
Notes:	

Website:	
Date:	
Username:	
Password:	
Notes:	

Website:	
Date:	
Username:	
Password:	
Notes:	

Website:	
Date:	
Username:	
Password:	
Notes:	

Website:	
Date:	
Username:	
Password:	
Notes:	

Website:	
Date:	
Username:	
Password:	
Notes:	

T

Website:	
Date:	
Username:	
Password:	
Notes:	

Website:	
Date:	
Username:	
Password:	
Notes:	

Website:	
Date:	
Username:	
Password:	
Notes:	

Website:	
Date:	
Username:	
Password:	
Notes:	

T

Website:	
Date:	
Username:	
Password:	
Notes:	

Website:	
Date:	
Username:	
Password:	
Notes:	

Website:	
Date:	
Username:	
Password:	
Notes:	

Website:	
Date:	
Username:	
Password:	
Notes:	

Website:	
Date:	
Username:	
Password:	
Notes:	

Website:	
Date:	
Username:	
Password:	
Notes:	

Website:	
Date:	
Username:	
Password:	
Notes:	

Website:	
Date:	
Username:	
Password:	
Notes:	

U

Website:	
Date:	
Username:	
Password:	
Notes:	

Website:	
Date:	
Username:	
Password:	
Notes:	

Website:	
Date:	
Username:	
Password:	
Notes:	

Website:	
Date:	
Username:	
Password:	
Notes:	

Website:	
Date:	
Username:	
Password:	
Notes:	

Website:	
Date:	
Username:	
Password:	
Notes:	

Website:	
Date:	
Username:	
Password:	
Notes:	

Website:	
Date:	
Username:	
Password:	
Notes:	

Website:	
Date:	
Username:	
Password:	
Notes:	

Website:	
Date:	
Username:	
Password:	
Notes:	

Website:	
Date:	
Username:	
Password:	
Notes:	

Website:	
Date:	
Username:	
Password:	
Notes:	

V

Website:	
Date:	
Username:	
Password:	
Notes:	

Website:	
Date:	
Username:	
Password:	
Notes:	

Website:	
Date:	
Username:	
Password:	
Notes:	

Website:	
Date:	
Username:	
Password:	
Notes:	

V

Website:	
Date:	
Username:	
Password:	
Notes:	

Website:	
Date:	
Username:	
Password:	
Notes:	

Website:	
Date:	
Username:	
Password:	
Notes:	

Website:	
Date:	
Username:	
Password:	
Notes:	

Website:	
Date:	
Username:	
Password:	
Notes:	

Website:	
Date:	
Username:	
Password:	
Notes:	

Website:	
Date:	
Username:	
Password:	
Notes:	

Website:	
Date:	
Username:	
Password:	
Notes:	

V

Website:	
Date:	
Username:	
Password:	
Notes:	

Website:	
Date:	
Username:	
Password:	
Notes:	

Website:	
Date:	
Username:	
Password:	
Notes:	

Website:	
Date:	
Username:	
Password:	
Notes:	

Website:	
Date:	
Username:	
Password:	
Notes:	

Website:	
Date:	
Username:	
Password:	
Notes:	

Website:	
Date:	
Username:	
Password:	
Notes:	

Website:	
Date:	
Username:	
Password:	
Notes:	

Website:	
Date:	
Username:	
Password:	
Notes:	

Website:	
Date:	
Username:	
Password:	
Notes:	

Website:	
Date:	
Username:	
Password:	
Notes:	

Website:	
Date:	
Username:	
Password:	
Notes:	

Website:	
Date:	
Username:	
Password:	
Notes:	

Website:	
Date:	
Username:	
Password:	
Notes:	

Website:	
Date:	
Username:	
Password:	
Notes:	

Website:	
Date:	
Username:	
Password:	
Notes:	

Website:	
Date:	
Username:	
Password:	
Notes:	

Website:	
Date:	
Username:	
Password:	
Notes:	

Website:	
Date:	
Username:	
Password:	
Notes:	

Website:	
Date:	
Username:	
Password:	
Notes:	

Website:	
Date:	
Username:	
Password:	
Notes:	

Website:	
Date:	
Username:	
Password:	
Notes:	

Website:	
Date:	
Username:	
Password:	
Notes:	

Website:	
Date:	
Username:	
Password:	
Notes:	

Website:	
Date:	
Username:	
Password:	
Notes:	

Website:	
Date:	
Username:	
Password:	
Notes:	

Website:	
Date:	
Username:	
Password:	
Notes:	

Website:	
Date:	
Username:	
Password:	
Notes:	

Website:	
Date:	
Username:	
Password:	
Notes:	

Website:	
Date:	
Username:	
Password:	
Notes:	

Website:	
Date:	
Username:	
Password:	
Notes:	

Website:	
Date:	
Username:	
Password:	
Notes:	

Website:	
Date:	
Username:	
Password:	
Notes:	

Website:	
Date:	
Username:	
Password:	
Notes:	

Website:	
Date:	
Username:	
Password:	
Notes:	

Website:	
Date:	
Username:	
Password:	
Notes:	

Y

Website:	
Date:	
Username:	
Password:	
Notes:	

Website:	
Date:	
Username:	
Password:	
Notes:	

Website:	
Date:	
Username:	
Password:	
Notes:	

Website:	
Date:	
Username:	
Password:	
Notes:	

Y

Website:	
Date:	
Username:	
Password:	
Notes:	

Website:	
Date:	
Username:	
Password:	
Notes:	

Website:	
Date:	
Username:	
Password:	
Notes:	

Website:	
Date:	
Username:	
Password:	
Notes:	

Y

Website:	
Date:	
Username:	
Password:	
Notes:	

Website:	
Date:	
Username:	
Password:	
Notes:	

Website:	
Date:	
Username:	
Password:	
Notes:	

Website:	
Date:	
Username:	
Password:	
Notes:	

Y

Website:	
Date:	
Username:	
Password:	
Notes:	

Website:	
Date:	
Username:	
Password:	
Notes:	

Website:	
Date:	
Username:	
Password:	
Notes:	

Website:	
Date:	
Username:	
Password:	
Notes:	

Z

Website:	
Date:	
Username:	
Password:	
Notes:	

Website:	
Date:	
Username:	
Password:	
Notes:	

Website:	
Date:	
Username:	
Password:	
Notes:	

Website:	
Date:	
Username:	
Password:	
Notes:	

Website:	
Date:	
Username:	
Password:	
Notes:	

Website:	
Date:	
Username:	
Password:	
Notes:	

Website:	
Date:	
Username:	
Password:	
Notes:	

Website:	
Date:	
Username:	
Password:	
Notes:	

Z

Website:	
Date:	
Username:	
Password:	
Notes:	

Website:	
Date:	
Username:	
Password:	
Notes:	

Website:	
Date:	
Username:	
Password:	
Notes:	

Website:	
Date:	
Username:	
Password:	
Notes:	

Website:	
Date:	
Username:	
Password:	
Notes:	

Website:	
Date:	
Username:	
Password:	
Notes:	

Website:	
Date:	
Username:	
Password:	
Notes:	

Website:	
Date:	
Username:	
Password:	
Notes:	

Printed in Great Britain
by Amazon